How to Become SuperStar Every Day

(The Secret of Life)

By

Khubah Khoirurobiq

Preface

This book guides you in your daily life so that you become a super star every day, wherever and any time. This book is suitable for all ages, because we use simple language and easy to understand for all ages.

If you are a student you are shy and difficult to penetrate the ranks of the most popular as well as well as academic ability, then the book is the solution.

If you are a young worker who still lack experience and you feel less confident about your ability to keep up with your work colleagues, then this is the book solution.

If you are a family and want a role model family your area, then this is the book solution.

Maybe you do not know me but believe that soon I will be a Super Star. How can this be? So the book is the solution.

Khubah Khoirurobiq

What do you see?

What do you see?

What do you see?

What do you see?

What do you see?

What do you see?

What do you see?

What do you see?

What do you see?

What do you see?

What do you see?

What do you see?

What do you see?

What do you see?

What do you see?

What do you see?

What do you see?

What do you see?

What do you see?

What do you see?

What do you see?

What do you see?

What do you see?

What do you see?

What do you see?

What do you see?

What do you see?

What do you see?

What do you see?

What do you see?

What do you see?

What do you see?

What do you see?

What do you see?

What do you see?

What do you see?

What do you see?

What do you see?

What do you see?

What do you see?

What do you see?

What do you see?

What do you see?

What do you see?

What do you see?

What do you see?

What do you see?

What do you see?

What do you see?

What do you see?

What do you see?

What do you see?

What do you see?

What do you see?

What do you see?

What do you see?

What do you see?

What do you see?

What do you see?

What do you see?

What do you see?

What do you see?

What do you see?

What do you see?

What do you see?

What do you see?

What do you see?

What do you see?

What do you see?

What do you see?

What do you see?

What do you see?

What do you see?

What do you see?

What do you see?

What do you see?

What do you see?

What do you see?

What do you see?

What do you see?

What do you see?

What do you see?

What do you see?

What do you see?

What do you see?

What do you see?

What do you see?

What do you see?

What do you see?

What do you see?

What do you see?

What do you see?

What do you see?

What do you see?

What do you see?

What do you see?

What do you see?

What do you see?

What do you see?

What do you see?

What do you see?

What do you see?

What do you see?

What do you see?

What do you see?

What do you see?

What do you see?

What do you see?

What do you see?

What do you see?

What do you see?

What do you see?

What do you see?

What do you see?

What do you see?

What do you

see?

What do you see?

What do you see?

What do you see?

What do you see?

What do you see?

What do you see?

What do you see?

What do you see?

What do you see?

What do you see?

What do you see?

What do you see?

What do you see?

What do you see?

What do you see?

What do you see?

What do you see?

What do you see?

What do you see?

What do you see?

What do you see?

What do you see?

What do you see?

What do you see?

What do you see?

What do you see?

What do you see?

What do you see?

What do you see?

What do you see?

What do you see?

What do you see?

What do you see?

What do you see?

After 150 page

Do you not see anything?

Do you not see anything?

Please check again!

Now what do you see?

If you still do not see anything?

Have a look again and see carefully.

You, you, you and you.

You are the only person who looks on the reflection page book, if you include the mirror above it.

What you think. Yourself is the secret itself. Yourself is the key to become a super star. Because you are a good man who is born in this world.

So now I enjoined you to look at this book every day so you remember that you are the best. You're the Super Star in the world.

Trust me!!! It's work

About the Author

Khubah Khoirurobiq is a human being. He opened a nobody and nothing. He's not a superstar or famous people. But he's got tremendous confidence to go ahead and move forward.

After completing his studies at the University Maiyah Nusantara, he tried to apply their knowledge in the field of life sciences. Because while studying at the University of Nusantara Maiyah she entered the Faculty of Life.

All this paper was inspired by a great teacher Nusantara University Maiyah IE Prop Cak Nun. Which has been in existence in the world of life.

10027883R00093

Printed in Great Britain
by Amazon.co.uk, Ltd.,
Marston Gate.